W9-COS-606

THE WEIGHT OF A LEAF

THE WEIGHT OF A LEAF

by
MYRA SCOVEL

THE WESTMINSTER PRESS
Philadelphia

Copyright © MCMLXX The Westminster Press

All rights reserved — no part of this book may be reproduced in any form without permission in writing from the publisher, except by a reviewer who wishes to quote brief passages in connection with a review in magazine or newspaper.

ISBN 0-664-20890-8

LIBRARY OF CONGRESS CATALOG CARD NO. 75-113471

ACKNOWLEDGMENTS

The author acknowledges to the following permission to reprint certain poems that first appeared in other publications:

American Weave: "Period Piece"
Baptist Leader: "He Knew"
Caravan (New Delhi): "Blind Man at the Taj Mahal"
Democrat and Chronicle (Rochester, New York): "Follow the Rain," "We Waken to Storm"
Imprints Quarterly: "After August," "Dialogue in a Spaceship," "Somewhere, a Peak"
Kaleidograph: "The Mountain Itself"
Mature Years: "To a Twelve-Year-Old"
New York Herald Tribune: "Branches for the Pyre," "Prerogative"
Outreach: "A Fir Stood Proudly"
Spirit: "Monastery Visitors' Room," "Ballade with a Double Refrain," "Sustenance"
The C. R. Gibson Company: *Garlands for Mother,* ed. by Ruth Wagner, "Gifts," "Interruption," "To a Twelve-Year-Old"
The Catholic Poetry Society *Bulletin:* "Interruption"
The Christian Century: "The Little Things," "Why Am I So Afraid?" "Marvel"

The Gleam (Annual of the Rochester, New York, Poetry Society): "To Li Po, Poet," "Deer in an Autumn Forest," "Stone Walls . . . ," "At the Catacombe di Sebastiane," "Branches for the Pyre," "Monastery Visitors' Room," "Creative Interlude," "Villanelle for Winter," "Attention, Please," "Prerogative," "Somewhere, a Peak," "Helen, Heaven"
The Lyric: "Dark Horse"
The Presbyterian Outlook for *The Presbyterian Tribune:* "Prayer Jubilant"
The Progressive Farmer: "Every Boy Should Have a Dog"
The Villager (Bronxville, New York): "First Monsoon Rain," "To a Friend Bereaved"
The Y.W.C.A. Magazine: "What Do They Do?"
Time for Singing: "Woodsmoke," "High Flight," "On Giving Up a Home"
Today: " 'So Is Every One That Is Born of the Spirit,' " " 'They Shall Renew Their Strength,' " "Lighting Candles"

Published by The Westminster Press ®
Philadelphia, Pennsylvania

PRINTED IN THE UNITED STATES OF AMERICA

For F., always,

and

TO LI PO, POET

Yellow the willow by your mountain pool,
one golden leaf following your skiff
as you painted brush strokes for these words
twelve hundred years ago.
　　"Shall goodwill ever be secure?
　　I watch the long road
　　of the River of Stars."

Grieved at the uselessness of war,
prey to the whims of court,
you were exiled to this quiet water.
Some say that you embraced the moon in it
and died.

Twelve hundred years, Li Po!
"Shall goodwill ever be secure?"
If it be true that you were drowned
in the silver of your sorrows,
you rose with the lotus, immortality,
dripping from your shoulders.

I, too, must watch, Li Po,
head raised to the long road
of the River of Stars.

THE WEIGHT OF A LEAF

Such Bounty

Dawn, in an Indian Temple

I Cannot Reach a Hand

After August

The Way Not Tried

Somewhere, a Peak

Contents

THE WEIGHT OF A LEAF

Such Bounty

THE WEIGHT OF A LEAF

We have bent to love
as a twig bends
to the weight of a leaf.

Together
we have felt the brush of wind,
learned where ripples
breathe under boulders,
listened for sounds
of a forest growing.

From the heat of fire,
the cold of stone,
fire and stone, stone and fire;
birth and death, death and rebirth,
has grown this forest —
has grown this love.

And from the bending
to the weight of a leaf.

DEER IN AN AUTUMN FOREST
[After an ancient Chinese painting]

Deer
stand motionless
in an eternal moment.
A doe,
lying in leaves,
curves
in a timeless ellipse.

Should one hoof strike stone,
it would ring down the silence
of ten thousand valleys.

"STONE WALLS..."

"Dear God," I cried,
before the gates clanged shut,
"However dark my cell may be,
grant that its window
frame a tree."

Lord, who am I
that Thou shouldst give
such bounty in reply —
pink ecstasy along a bough,
spring against sky!

16

AT THE CATACOMBE DI SEBASTIANE

He ran,
a hunted thing
across the fields from Rome.

His sandaled feet
cut arrows through the grass;
poppies were whipped aside
as he passed.

These catacombs
became his home.
Upon these walls
he wrote his prayer:
    "Paul and Peter,
    pray for Victor."

Reaping the harvest
of his sunless years,
I, too, pray:
    "Paul and Peter,
    thank him, Victor."

Dawn, in an Indian Temple

DAWN, IN AN INDIAN TEMPLE

My Lord,
I come to worship Thee.
I come
bringing one lotus and one rose
from Thy world.

I cannot find Thee in the world.
I am troubled by the plethora of roses,
bewildered by the many-flowered pools.

Let me lay the fragments of my life
before Thee.
Only here
can I become whole.

FORGIVE EMPTY HANDS

Forgive empty hands.
I cannot tear the flowers
to petal Thy feet.

FIRST MONSOON RAIN

Softly
a sigh is blown,
scuttering leaves into the night.

Suddenly
the crisp crack of the lightning's whip
stings the sky
and the rain (oh, is it rain?) begins.

Across the land
in one lithe movement,
men open their doors,
breathe in the mixture of drought and damp,
lift their faces to feel the drops,
smile at the dappling dust at their feet,
grateful
for dappling dust.

BLIND MAN AT THE TAJ MAHAL

The worn hand trembled on the stalwart shoulder.
"Tell me what it's like," the old man said.
"Four massive doors, each carved from one huge boulder,
and here the tomb which holds the ancient dead.
Four marble minarets . . ." The young voice faltered.
Where are the words for one who cannot see?
The very telling leaves perfection altered,
cutting deep scars across its symmetry.
"There is a fragile dome, a molded tear,
holding itself against the sky above
by some sheer power of beauty, past belief.
It is a vessel . . . words make nothing clear . . .
a vessel shaped upon the wheel of love,
baked in the hottest kiln, the kiln of grief."

BRANCHES FOR THE PYRE

Climb the tree and break each brittle bough.
Gather the bitter fuel nor ponder how
the wind through pine could be her last long sigh.
Gather the bitter fuel and pile it high,
nor stay to sob, hot head against cool bark,
seeing the inevitable flame across the dark.
Gather the frantic fuel and pile it high,
nor speak . . . , nor cry.

I Cannot Reach a Hand

TO A FRIEND BEREAVED

I cannot reach a hand to touch your sorrow.
I sit alone this fading afternoon
wishing I could tell you that tomorrow
spring would come. Instead the winter moon
may slowly mist with ice the grief you're bearing
and autumn will have gone her way too soon.
If I could take the fire she is wearing,
if I could take the splendor of her gold
or know the quiet courage of her daring
to flaunt her leaves, so soon to turn to mold,
how clearly you would see her allegory!
But as I face with you the coming cold,
the valiant leaves flash through the hills *their* story.
Beloved, they go out aflame with glory.

THE ARTIST

"Too weak to storm success,"
they taunted —
they,
swept up by the turbulent stream.

How could they know
the courage it had taken
to defy the current,
to struggle through the clinging mud
to this bleak room
with half its windows gone?

Light, you had here;
light was all you needed
for color, flung in affirmation
across your canvases.

Light
was all you felt you needed.
Light, you had
and light you gave.

THE NAPKIN, FOLDED

She does not know that you have gone away.
Faithful soul, she lays the place for two.
She takes the breakfast bacon from the tray
and wonders what can be delaying you.
I smile and say that you will soon return.
(No actor ever played a better part.)
She says her daily, "Oh, my bread will burn!"
and hurries out, wheeling the old tea cart.

The time will come when she will have to know —
the time when I shall have to come to grips
with life, or what will have to pass for such.
Now, for this moment, I must let tears flow,
touching the silver that your hand would touch,
holding the napkin that should brush your lips.

MONASTERY VISITORS' ROOM

Now that our greetings are over,
silence has fallen.
I note you are wearing
my favorite color.
I lay fresh wood on the fire,
smooth out the folds of my cassock.
Together we watch the fingers of flame
caress the rough jowls of a log.

Ah, but once this log
was alive in the forest outside,
a tree that storms could not tame.
I must see
that only the casual words are said —
that no spark is kindled.

"Is it too late?" you ask,
and the plumes on your small hat quiver.
"Have you so quickly forgotten?"

How can I tell you
that yours is a flame
that would burn me to ash?
You would not know of the bush ablaze
with a fire that never consumes.

FOR YOU, LYING THERE

You, of all persons, did not need to be
brought low before your loved to this degree.
I rail against the fumbling of your hands,
your mutterings that once were clear commands.
The God above, you say, must have his reasons
for giving man his bleak and fruitful seasons.
Spring, summer, autumn, yes; but not December —
not your stripped look when striving to remember;
not stains spilled down your vest, crumbs on your lips,
someone to lift what once were virile hips.
Do not speak of such a God to me.
Unless spring comes for you, what blasphemy!
If seed-break-sod for you has no relation,
death is but one vast humiliation.

THE HOUSE IS QUIET

No sun
streams through the window;
no bird sings.
The house is quiet
like the grave
in which he sleeps;

like the grave
in which his body sleeps.
He is alive with golden sun;
he is the song
of all birds singing.

The house is quiet
like the tomb
in which I cannot sleep.

After August

AFTER AUGUST

There are elements of mystery now
on every hand.
Why but one scarlet pennant
flying from a grove of maples?
Who decided, overnight,
which leaf to daub with yellow?
And who trailed a torn, brown remnant
across that field of green?

CREATIVE INTERLUDE

Frost lies soft
along the furrows of a mind
fallow now,
after the fecund summer.

To drift, weightless,
light as the empty pods of winter,
is all the ecstasy a mind can hold
after a fevered harvest.

VILLANELLE FOR WINTER

How quietly the shadows go
across our bleak and barren tree;
how silent is the fall of snow!

Today no solitary crow
lights heavily and waits to see
how quietly the shadows go,

or if that bright and sparkling glow
will break into a symphony.
How silent is the fall of snow —

so still we cannot hear the flow
of moments left for you and me
as quietly the shadows go.

Had we noticed, could we know
(with life so full of melody)
how silent is the fall of snow?

Do we still have time? If so,
love will teach us patiently,
as quietly the shadows go,
how silent is the fall of snow.

SECURE WITHIN THIS LEAFY TOMB

Closed in by summer, I forget
an urgency beyond this gloom —
the cry of peaks unclimbed as yet.

This season of the year's quartette
is meant for nestling in the womb.
Closed in by summer, I forget.

No far horizon looms to whet
an appetite for chancing doom,
no cry of peaks unclimbed as yet.

Will I be stifled by regret
and will the womb become the tomb
closed in by summer? I forget

the goals I once so bravely set.
Who spurs me on? From whom
the cry of peaks unclimbed as yet?

Strike through this lethargy's thick net!
Push back the plethora of bloom!
Closed in by summer, I forget
the cry of peaks unclimbed as yet.

FOLLOW THE RAIN

I hear the rain leave the forest;
I see it stipple the lake.
Three notes of a birdcall
come in its wake.

But I remain in the cabin,
fearing the lake exposed
to sun and an open heaven.
Doors must be closed.

Rain and bird leave the forest.
Both are wiser than I;
rain to become seawater,
bird to reach sky.

The Way Not Tried

THE LITTLE THINGS

Under the leaves
there is a world
of scurrying things.

Lift a leaf
and there is a sudden darting
into subterranean passages —
a scramble for the dark.

With a cover of leaves
the little things
are not afraid of being trampled;
little things have always been trampled.

It is light
they fear.

OLD BATTLEFIELD

I

Stern outcroppings of rock
are ludicrous
when the dogwood is in bloom.
Cannon are lost in froth;
markers —
"Two companies of the British . . ."
(heaven and the Queen be spared)
are framed in lace.

II

The museum guard is taking a breather.
Tired of his faded photographs,
cases of charred nails,
rusty chain and old medals,
he puffs his pipe
under ballet skirts stiff with bloom.

III

"Where did all these trees come from?
Who planted them?" someone asks.

"It's kind of a Johnny Appleseed story."
He pushes back his cap,
shifts his squint from the sun.
"Young chap from over east, I've heard tell,
got sick of the fighting during the Civil War.
Looked around
for the prettiest thing he could find
to bring back north.
Planted them all over this part of the country."

IV

One blossom
covering the hand
of a black child.
"Look, Amarylla,
did you ever see anything
so white?"

"It's white, all right, Carrie,
but what's that stain
around the edge?"

SO GAY THE CARNIVAL

The tree
where the feeder hangs
is a pinwheel of color.

Birds
in the spangled snow
are chirring a merry-go-round.

So gay the carnival
one forgets
that hunger turns the cárrousel.

ATTENTION, PLEASE

Afraid to fall, lest we be trampled,
we are all lost, here —
lost in the scramble of "What will it cost?"
trapped in the maze of "Come what may,
she shall have the hat and the shoes
and the purse and the gloves that I never had."

The salesmen are lost;
hiding themselves behind bushes of tissue
and boxes of shoes.
A salesgirl is lost in a billow of blouses,
the undertow dragging her down.

We know we are lost,
having by now
become used to our lostness.

But what of the child?
"Attention, please.
Will the parents of Linda Lou Sacks
come to the cosmetic counter?
Repeating,
a child in pink, about four years of age;
she calls herself Linda Lou Sacks,
or something like that.
Will the parents of Linda Lou Sacks
come to the cosmetic counter?
Attention, please. Repeating . . ."

What will Easter mean
to a lost child,
screaming at pink, patent leather, and straw?
"I told you I wanted elevens."
"Give me that blouse with the beads;
it'll go nice with the hat."

　　　Linda, there is a garden,
　　　a tomb, deserted.
　　　How will you find Him
　　　who *died* for the lost?

WE HAD OFTEN SPOKEN IDLY

We had often spoken idly
of what it would be like
to be the last two people left on earth.
How little we knew!

How *little* we knew that morning
when we went into the shelter of old roofing
you'd hastily constructed
so we could "sugar off"!

Fragments of that hour
are separate etchings on my tired brain —
the buckets, hung against the maples,
were brimful of sun;
icicles, lazily trying to form
and finding it not worth the effort,
dripped methodically,
each drop a sphere until it reached the snow.
I remember how the melting crusts
began to look like isinglass,
how the air had a slight bouquet of cider.

You were quoting Scott
as you squelched back and forth in your heavy boots,
feeding fuel to the fire.
> "Despite his title, power and pelf,
> the wretch, concentered . . ."

Did the quotation end?
Did we see the dreaded cloud?
Did we hear the blast?
I don't know.

We wakened to this tortured, twisted
photograph from LIFE.
All we'd known
had been masticated by some Machiavellian Metabolism
and spewn out before our eyes.

It cannot be much longer now.
Hold me again.
The only comfort I have
is your tobacco-permeated Irish tweed.
How pure, how clean it smells
in this sick stench of death.

DIALOGUE IN A SPACESHIP

". . . It would take a thousand years to reach the nearest star. . . . How much more efficient to send only the human cells, to fertilize them automatically twenty years before the voyage was due to end . . ." — *Science News Note.*

She: This table is so smooth.
　　　 Somewhere in my memory, wood is rough.
　　　 And in this cold, dark world
　　　 through which we move,
　　　 I dream of . . . sun.

He: What is sun?

She: I don't know,
　　　 nor why I said the word,
　　　 as when you said "song."
　　　 Sun. I feel it when you hold me.

He: I, too, have dreams.
　　　 I'm on a ship — but not this ship.
　　　 There's a throbbing through the prow
　　　 like the throbbing through your breast.
　　　 A hundred fingers lift my hair,
　　　 and when I taste the spray across my face
　　　　 I'm not surprised your tears are . . .

She: Salt?

MEDITATION IN A FACTORY

This little stamp
on this little disk
endlessly endless,
     stamp, click,
     stamp, click,
this is my life
endlessly clicking away.

What is this disk
that I make all day?
How is it used?
     Stamp, click,
     stamp, click,
one little disk
ticking my life away.

Is it one little note
to complete a scroll
of the music of God;
     stamp, click,
     stamp, click,
the one little disk
making eternity whole?

THE WAY NOT TRIED

Shorten all vowels
until speech becomes Disney's duck;
train eyes to keep pace
with the spew of presses;
feed rats new drugs
to increase the brain's convolutions;
the more knowledge gulped,
the more there will be to gorge.

Put *me* down for research
on the way not tried.
Let me listen
for the sound of one leaf
loosening from its stem;
trace the shadows
trees let fall across snow;
taste the sun in tart berries.

Let me marvel
at the holy order of dawn.

PREROGATIVE

Hands cupped
over the quivering flame,
we make our choice.
We, the guardians, will be to blame
if a cold gust
leaves us no voice.

Our hands tremble
as we shield the light.
How can we choose?
God, give us wisdom;
there is much to lose.

Somewhere, a Peak

SOMEWHERE, A PEAK

I cannot live on this island.
I am mocked by spume,
battered by relentless rhythm,
sucked dry
by the recoil of waves spent.

Somewhere
there is a mountain
whose jagged rocks
are stirrups for my climb;

somewhere, a peak
so vibrant with silence
that I will hear my name.

WHY AM I SO AFRAID?

Why am I so afraid
to let God speak?
He will want me to throw out
the rubbish from my life,
all the dear, accumulated rubbish.

He will clean me out,
down to the bare essentials of my being.
I am afraid,
afraid of that nakedness.

"IF I MAKE MY BED IN SHEOL, THOU ART THERE"

So I read.
But I cannot find Thee,
O unembraceable God.

I kneel
longing to bow my head to Thy feet.
In vain, I search for tangible hands.

If my heart swells to encompass the world,
space, and the space beyond space,
I cannot touch Thee.

What hast Thou done, O my God —
Thou who hast dealt us the hunger
of a love we can never give?

APRIL FOOL

April again,
cold, sodden April;
and I have had my fill
of plastic daffodils.

Then am I such a fool
that, seeing a fern fist break sod,
once more I believe in God?

"SO IS EVERY ONE THAT IS BORN OF THE SPIRIT"

"Where does the wind come from, Nicodemus?"
"Rabbi, I do not know."
"Nor can you tell where it will go.

"Put yourself into the path of the wind,
Nicodemus.
You will be borne along
by something greater than yourself.
You are proud of your position,
content in your security,
but you will perish in such stagnant air.

"Put yourself into the path of the wind,
Nicodemus.
Bright leaves will dance before you.
You will find yourself in places
you never dreamed of going;
you will be forced into situations
you have dreaded
and find them like a coming home.

"You will have a power you never had before,
Nicodemus.
You will be a new man.
Put yourself into the path of the wind."

HE KNEW

"... and now they were not able to draw it for the multitude of fishes. Therefore that disciple . . . saith unto Peter, It is the Lord." — *John 21: 6-7.*

He knew.
How few there are
who do.

With nets
so silver-seething full,
our one regret —
the sea holds more,
the sea holds more.

How easy to forget
that Figure on the shore,
accepting as our due
the breaking net
without the happy shout,
"It is the Lord!"

PETER REMEMBERS

That night He said to me
across the snarling lake,
"Come."
And I started out,
never dreaming that I might not make it.
There He stood, smiling a bit,
as He so often did,
and I smiled back and walked along that lake
as if it were a country road.
As long as I kept my eyes on Him
it was fun.
But for some fool reason
I started looking down instead of up.
Panic? That's a small word
when you find yourself in the midst
of a howling sea!
"What am I doing here?" I wanted to know.
"This just can't be! Nobody ever did this before!"
I began to sink.

"THEY SHALL RENEW THEIR STRENGTH"

They who wait,
who stand stock-still
amid the whir of wheels,
refusing to be crushed,
can never be enslaved;
cannot be bound to a relentless clock
swung round and round,
hearing no other sound
but time's tick-tock.

They who wait
become imbued with strength,
swing the wide reach of sky
on sure, swift wings;
run with exuberance
through sun-splashed fields;
walk on with single-purposed feet,
walk on, and do not faint.

YOU KNOW, LORD

Lord, today I am afraid
to take one step alone.

You know
how I go blundering through life,
trampling the flowers
of another's sowing,
breaking open the all-but-healed wounds
of another's sorrow,
bludgeoning my way through
to what *I* think should be done . . .

You leave me today
at Your own risk, Lord.
You know so well
what I am without You.

LIGHTING CANDLES

"All the darkness in the world
cannot put out the light of one small candle."

In this still hour
God holds his great lamp low
that I may light my prayers.

Shining through the world they go,
one here, one there.
No "curtain" can keep out their glow;
no heart so cold
it cannot feel their loving warmth.
The world is being changed tonight.

Lit at the lamp of God
in this still hour,
prayer
is lighting candles everywhere.

MARVEL

A cardinal caught fire
in the setting sun.
Strange, that in all that glory
neither bird nor I
was consumed.

GOD SAID

And all the time
there was sky above you,
there was birdsong and laughter,
rain and healing sun;
there was warm, abiding comfort
for your sorrow,
there were friends, color,
work to do, home.

It was a world in which
each new tomorrow held surprise.
It was the heaven
that you would not see;
it was Heaven
and you would not lift your eyes.

FAMILY PORTRAIT

Like Coming Home

*The Children, Scarlet-sweatered
from the Cold*

Love Is More than Words

Contents

FAMILY PORTRAIT

Love Is More than Words

Like Coming Home

SO YOUR VOICE

A light wind
brushing the poplar grove
starts but one leaf
shaking.

Dawn,
gold on her fingertip,
touches one bird
waking.

So your voice
in this crowded room
leaves one heart
quaking.

PRAYER JUBILANT

Father, I must speak to You
in some secluded place tonight.
Shut me in quietly with You alone.
I cannot step into the expanse
of this bounty;
I dare not face
the blessing You have given.
Shut me in quietly with You alone
and give me strength to meet
the joy, the joy, the joy!

A BRIDE, ON SEEING HER WEDDING GIFTS

Lovely, shining things, you are as new
as this bright feeling in me.
Such untried, unused loveliness!
Will it mellow into soft, familiar oldness?
And will our love, so scintillating now?

DARK HORSE

I thought you'd be a hero in bright armor
and ride a steed as black as yonder bough.
Bellérophon turned out to be a farmer
and Pegasus is there beside the plow.
I dreamed that you would snatch me from the dragons
and through the fragrant world we two would roam.
I didn't know brides ever rode on wagons —
that love was very much like coming home.

Am I not, then, content with all before me?
I see hurt cross your face at this surmise.
Beloved, two upon one horse would bore me,
and Galahad himself I would not prize.
Your jacket is so comfortable and old;
embracing armor could be very cold.

THIS STRONG DEATH

Sleep is strong enough
to cut an end to day,
to sweep into oblivion
the disarray
of masks and clutter.

Sleep can snap the will to do,
twist the steel of scheme,
slam shut the door
to project, plan, and plot.

Strange, that at dawn we smile,
our lives unchanged by this strong death,
our love untouched.

WE WAKEN TO STORM

We waken to storm this morning,
wind and rain pelting the roof
like schoolboys.
The old rooms chuckle and shake,
every rafter
creaking a joke in reply.

Whorls of happiness ribbon the lawn.
We are caught up by song
that has swept us without any warning.
Laughter is loose on the world.

The Children,
Scarlet-sweatered
from the Cold

WOODSMOKE

Woodsmoke on an autumn afternoon,
   a bonfire and the air like applejack,
eager tongues of flame that lick the spoon
   of brown leaf batter and the crisp crack
of twigs the tint of cinnamon sticks. Soon
   three-thirty chatter and a bookbag's "thwack" —
the children, scarlet-sweatered from the cold,
tumble home from school knee-deep in gold.

A
fir
stood
proudly
in the wood
outlined by sky.
A child cried, "Look,
the stars are all caught
in
it.
God has made us
a Christmas tree!"

WHAT DO THEY DO?

What do they do
on blissful days like this,
these poor who have no God?

When autumn sets a torch to every tree,
when ecstasy
would all but burst the heart,
what do they do,
with no one to say thank you to!

HIGH FLIGHT

Mounting a sunset sky,
the kite
tips and swerves,
wavers and turns,
lunges, lonely in flight.

And you
tug at the strings,
hungry for wings.

EVERY BOY SHOULD HAVE A DOG

Every boy should have a dog.
I've had it drummed into my ears
continually for seven years.
Of course, a boy should have a dog.

I have succumbed to pleading eye,
to smudge of mud on quivering chin,
his hopeful father joining in
to tell again the reasons why.

And now I find this muff of joy
that chews his shoes, that licks his face,
has proved beyond the slightest trace
that every dog should have a boy.

GIFTS

Could anything in all God's world
be sweeter than this pile of baby clothes!
Cream woolly shirts like golden fleece,
soft muslins edged with shells of lace,
pink sweaters with their bonnets round
to frame her face;
the finely woven blankets
so meant for cuddling,
and Grandma's cashmere "double gown"
featherstitched with love.

HELEN, HEAVEN

Helen,
a petal of roses
from heaven;

Helen, a shell
from the heavenly shore;

petal of roses
and delicate shell,
Helen is more.

Dimpled,
in dimity,
Helen
is pure personality.

But seven days old,
Helen is more than a shell or a rose;
she wrinkles the daintiest elf of a nose
and eternity
stirs at our door.

HOW DID THE WORLD GET SO CLEAN, MOTHER?

God washed the day
and hung it out to dry,
dripping with dew.

Sun shone,
wind blew.

When evening came,
the cherubs,
pink from play,
folded it with lavender
to put away.

INTERRUPTION

How can I write a poem
with you two there at the door,
watching me every moment,
asking questions galore?

Do you remember the artist,
Raphael was his name,
who painted as cherubs the urchins
who played at his window frame?

Now if you two are determined
to keep running in all the time,
you *may* find yourselves, my darlings,
with your heads sticking out of a rhyme.

TO A TWELVE-YEAR-OLD

Tell me what you're thinking of —
Priam's war, your latest love,
how they make a rocket go,
the game, or last night's TV show?

Are you many miles away
digging gold in old Pompeii,
or are you somewhat nearer home,
gliding from the courthouse dome?

Perhaps you're someone very great
whose word decides the nation's fate.
I'd like so much to catch your eye;
I've said three times, "Please pass the pie."

ALL SOULS' EVE

Halloween candy world,
    the moon a grinning pumpkin,
where scarecrow trees and shocks of corn
    play the bumpkin;

earth in hilarious mask,
    soon to don ghostly sheets,
you will take love and love alone.
    Will it be tricks or treats?

BALLADE WITH A DOUBLE REFRAIN

What of a son whose chief delight
   is to change the world in a single day?
How do you cope with his love to fight?
    He cannot accept an expedient way,
    and only half listens to all we say.
There are stars in his eyes for the battle half won;
    with a sword in his hand he is in it to stay.
What do you do with a difficult son?

He worries a lot about black versus white,
    and is very concerned for the poor émigré.
At once he must see that all is made right;
    he cannot accept an expedient way.
    Why won't he buy a guitar and play,
take out some girls and join in the fun?
    But no, he must see that man from Bombay.
What do you do with a difficult son?

Concerning our country, he's very contrite.
    There are certain phases he plans to survey.
His findings will all be simply airtight.
    He cannot accept an expedient way.
    How he loves to pull off a neat exposé!
We should have stopped him before he'd begun.
    It's one of the reasons why mothers get gray.
What do you *do* with a difficult son?

L'ENVOI

Mary, Mother of God, I pray,
(He cannot accept an expedient way)
Give wisdom and courage, O Knowing One,
What did they do with Your Difficult Son!

GO WHERE YOU WILL

Go where you will across the world,
you cannot reach a point beyond our love.
But do not fear,
love can never play the rope
to let you go, to draw you near;
let love be the wings on which you soar.

Love Is More than Words

PERIOD PIECE

The road winds on
over the hill to the Hewlett farm.
Once or twice a month,
years ago,
we Wyants saddled up
and went to talk
of butter, eggs, and calico.

We spent the day.
The men went out to see the hay
while Sarah put the chicken on to fry.

I wonder why,
now that the car
would speed us to their door,
we never see the Hewletts anymore.

CAREER WOMAN

Do they know,
they in my brittle, paper-clipped world,
that behind the efficient facade,
a quivering wife
waits for the strength of your hand?

SUSTENANCE

"Love is bread," they said.
"Love is salt.
Love is a bitter load
come winter weather."

But bread is sweet;
salt is a need.
The load, we bear together
down any road,
come any weather.

"AND GOD SHALL WIPE AWAY ALL TEARS"

She stepped out of the yellow-curtained room
that happy, golden morning,
crossed her garden
with its dew-teared flowers
and low caressing trees,
to the door of that dear Other House.

How radiant she was!
How glad to find
each loved one there to meet her,
as God took her by the hand and said,
"At last you've come.
Beloved, welcome home."

ON GIVING UP A HOME

A house should not outlive its usefulness;
a mother bird deserts her empty nest
and soars to new horizons on brave wing,
too wise to reminisce.

Bird, I dare not look, as I go out,
at morning glories growing by a swing.

THE MOUNTAIN ITSELF

Silence
covers the mountain like a cloud.
Wind, brushing the grass,
is not sound;
it is only an added stillness.

Here in the quiet,
I know again that love is more than words.
It is not the wind but the silence;
not the wild orchids in the grass,
but the mountain itself.

MYRA SCOVEL

MYRA SCOVEL is the wife of Dr. Frederick Gilman Scovel, Acting Medical Director for United Presbyterian work overseas. For twenty-one years the Scovels were medical missionaries in China. (Mrs. Scovel is an R.N.) It was in China that Mrs. Scovel first began to write poetry seriously, at the insistence of her husband, who "promised me break-fast in bed any Saturday that I would have a poem on his desk by noon."

During the Sino-Japanese War, the Scovels lived for six years within the sound of gunfire, once near enough for Dr. Scovel to be wounded seriously. The Scovels and their five children were interned by the Japanese in a camp at Weihsien, Shantung. Repatriated on the last trip the *Gripsholm* made from the Orient, the family arrived in New York on December 1, 1943, whereupon Mrs. Scovel was rushed immediately to the hospital to give birth to their sixth child.

The Scovels returned to China in 1946. When the Communists took over Canton, Dr. Scovel was teaching in Ling Nan Medical College. He and his wife remained at their work for another year and a half, until their position became untenable. They were then sent by their church to India, where Dr. Scovel became Professor of Medicine at the Ludhiana Christian Medical College, and Mrs. Scovel began work on her first prose book, *The Chinese Ginger Jars*. They are now living in Stony Point, New York. Mrs. Scovel continues her career as a writer of both prose and poetry. "But my first love has always been poetry," she says.